At the

Alan A. Rubin
Illustrated by Helle Urban

Rigby®
A Harcourt Achieve Imprint

www.Rigby.com
1-800-531-5015

Look at the pond.

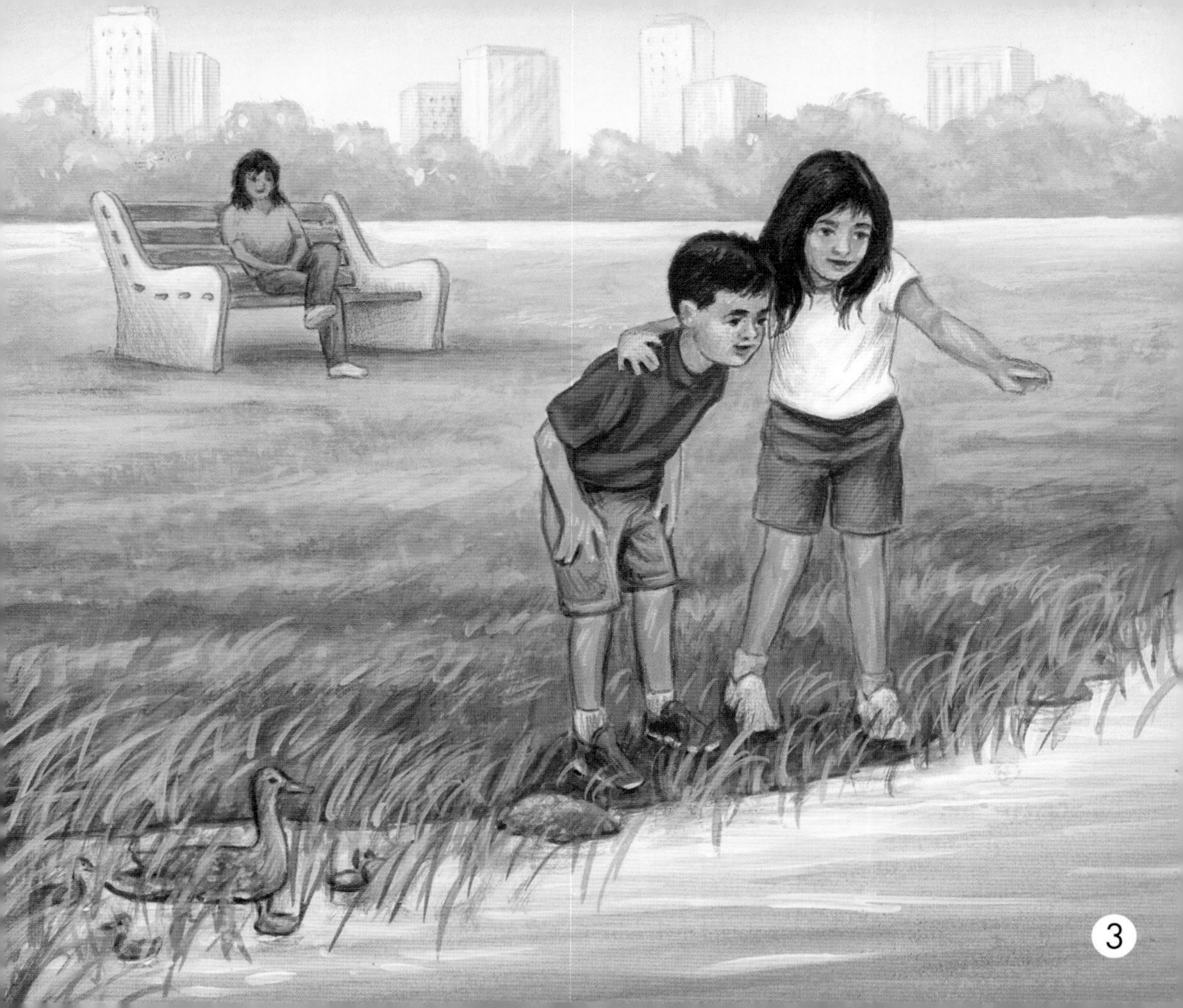

Look at the ducks!

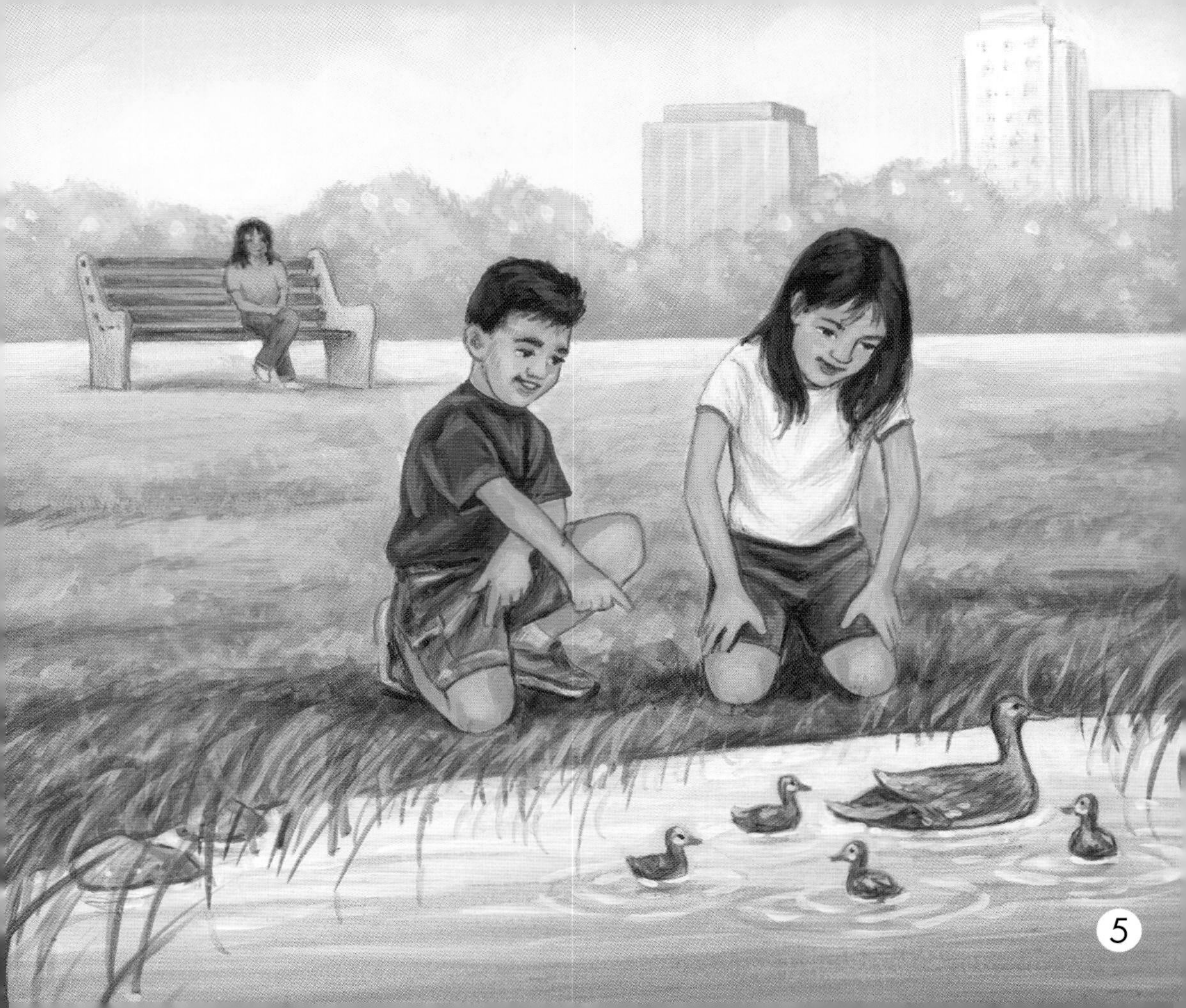

Look at the log.

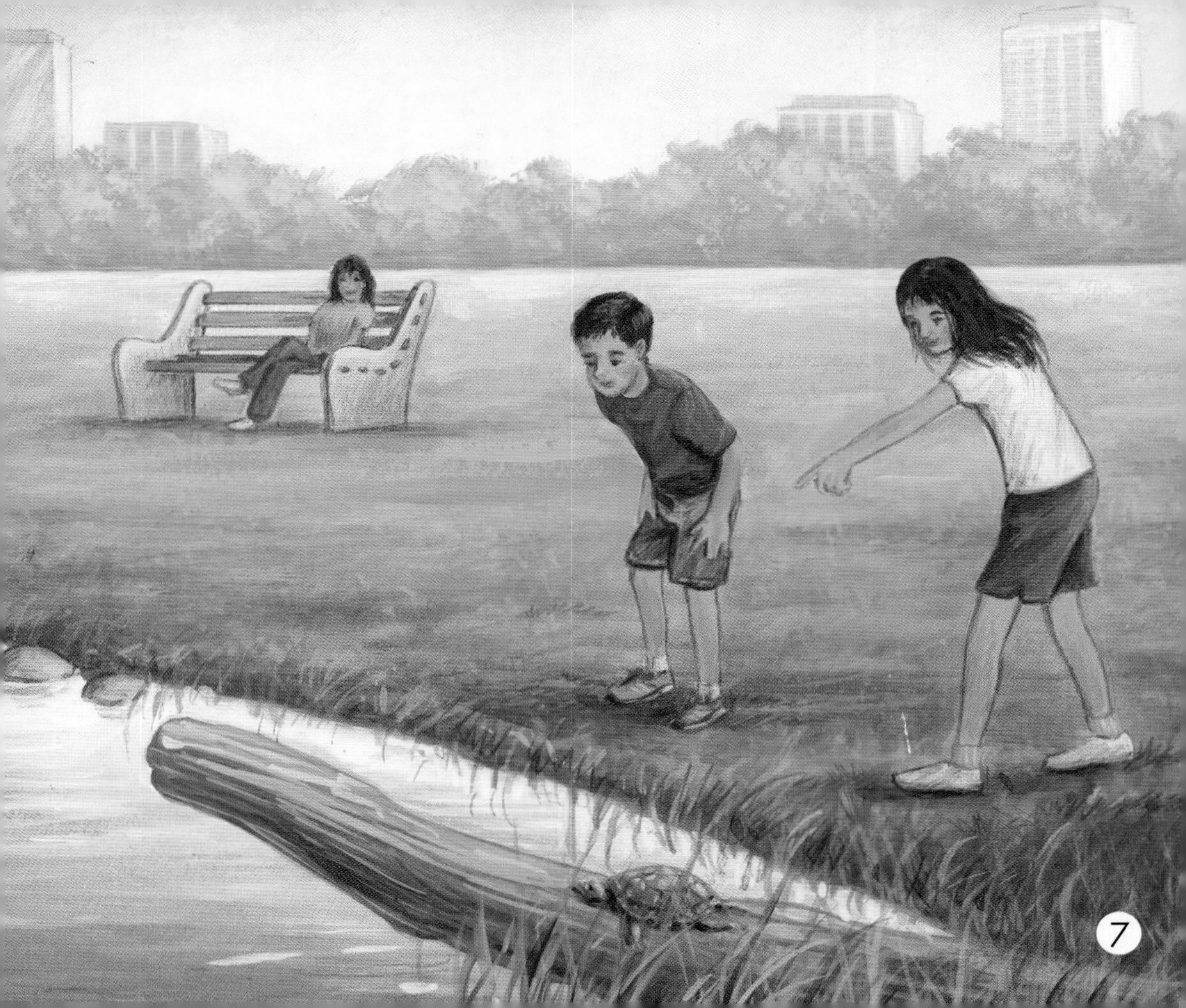

Look at the turtle!

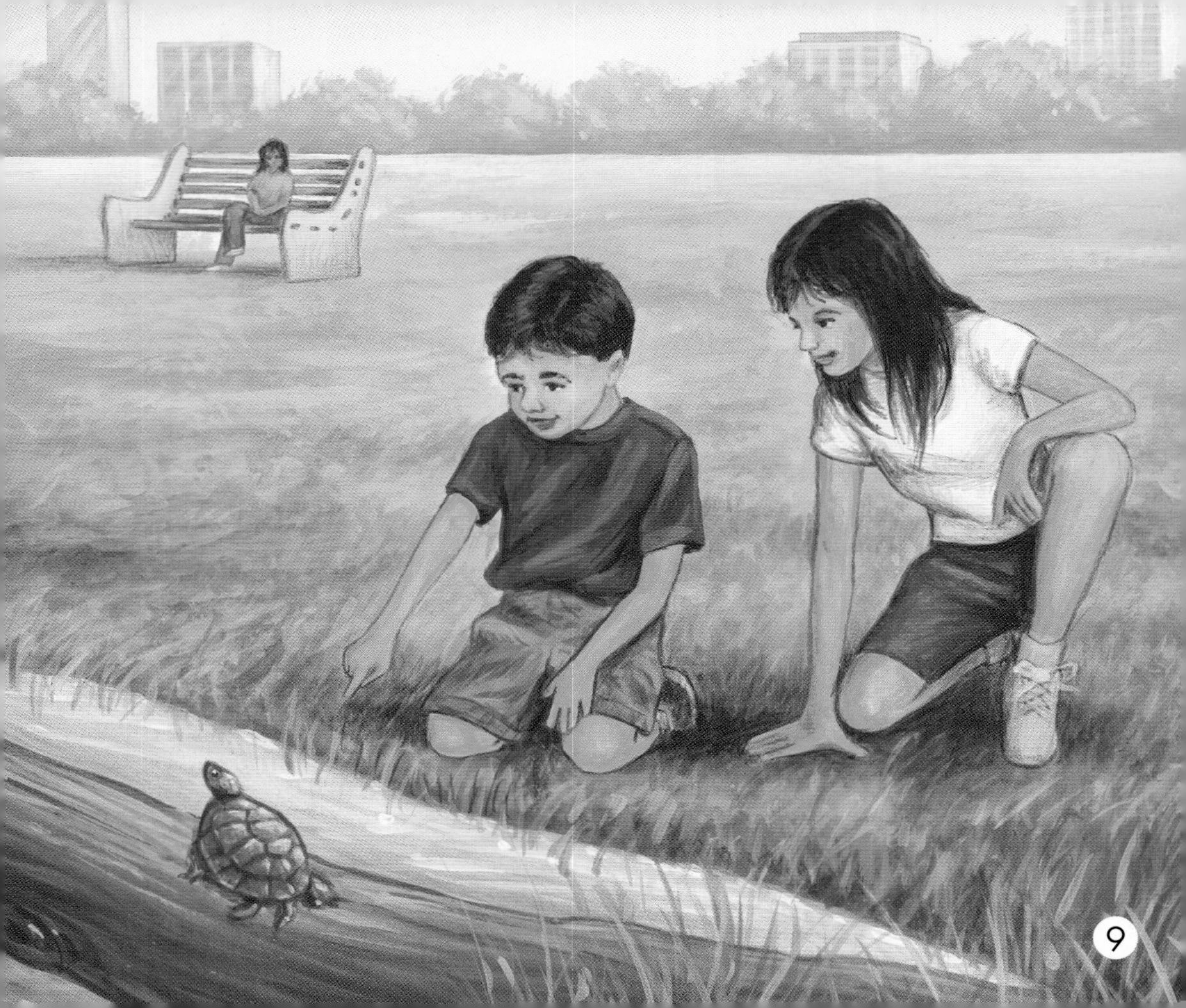

Look at the boat.

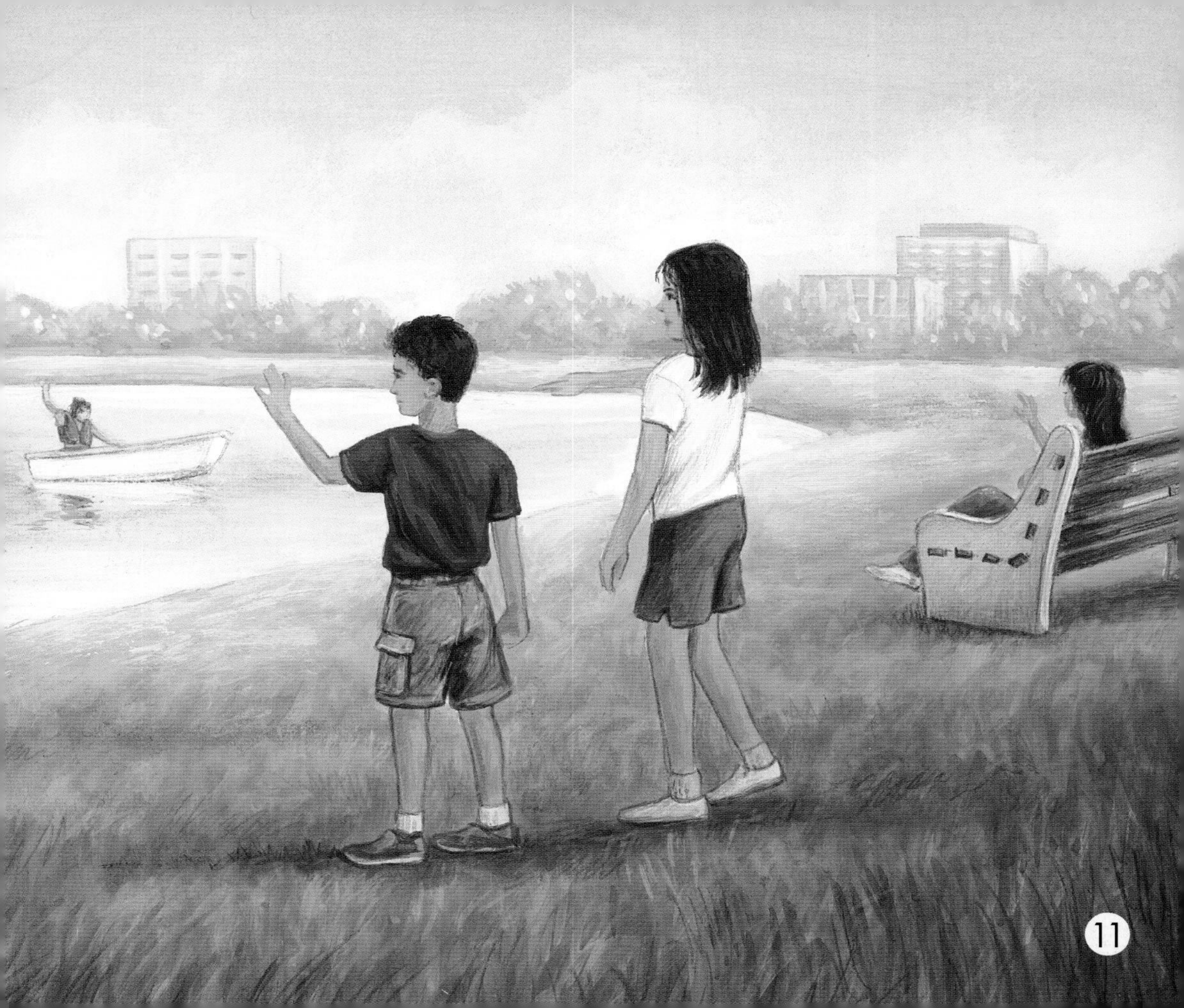

Look at the fish!

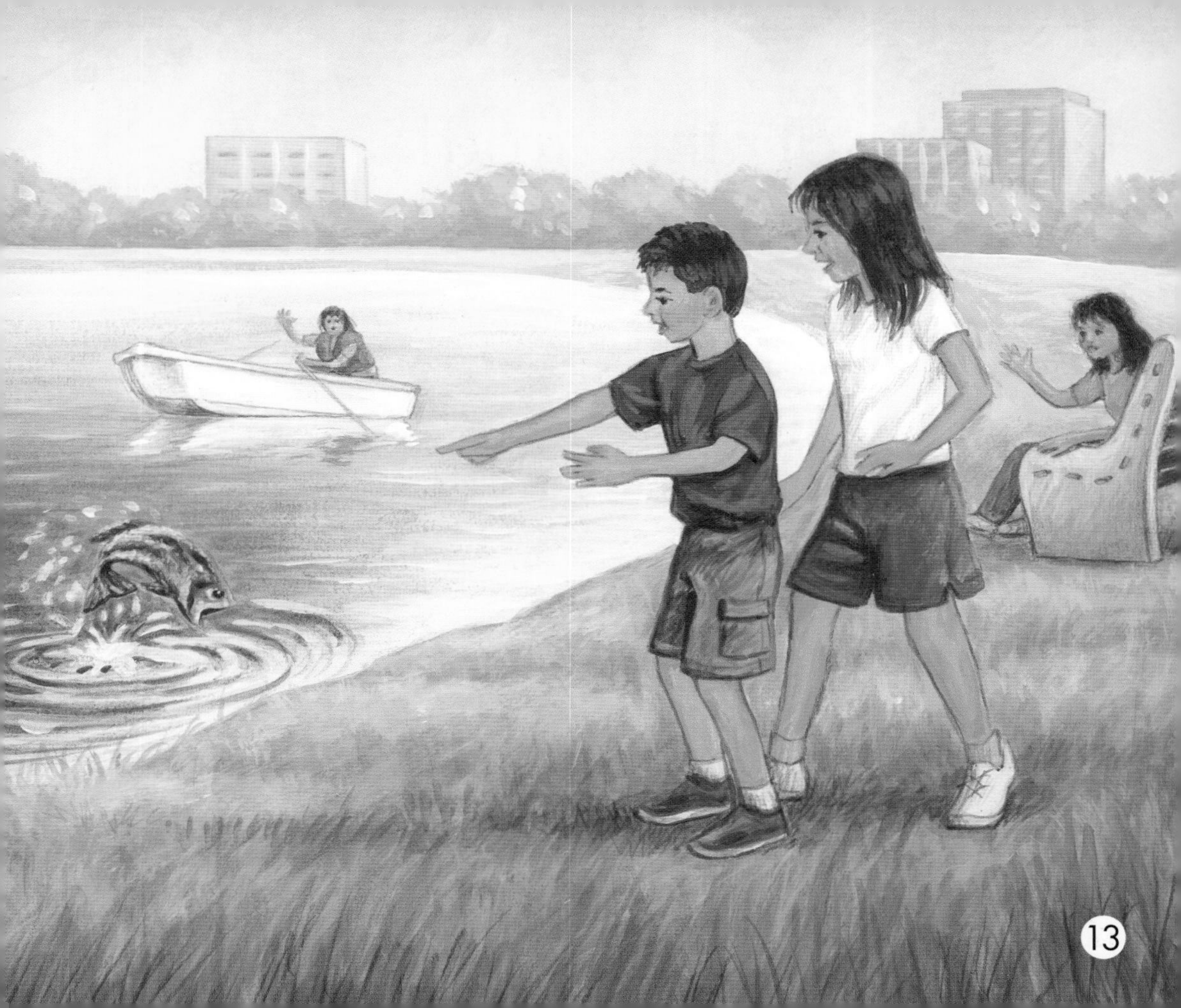

Look at the frog!

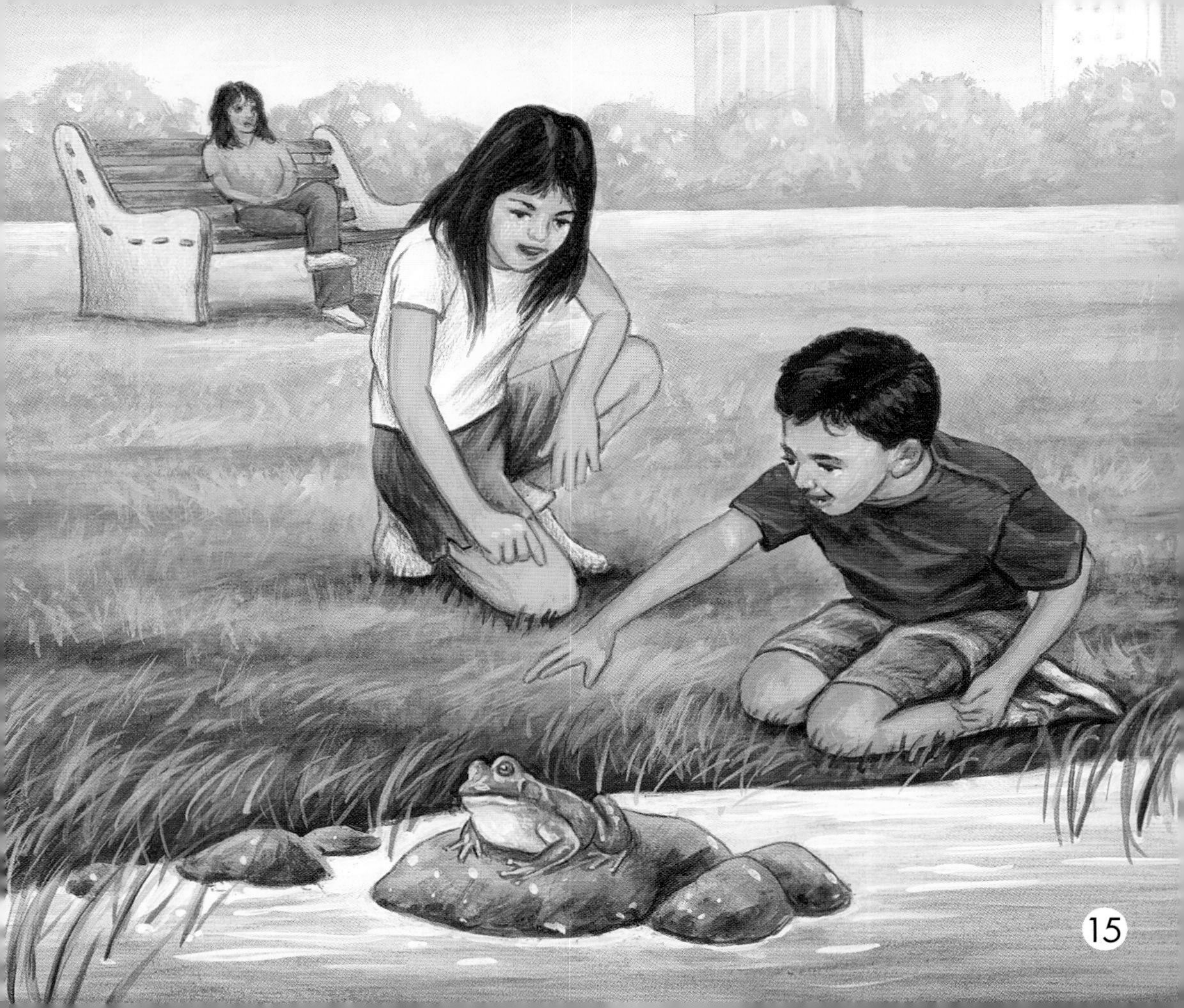

Look at the splash!

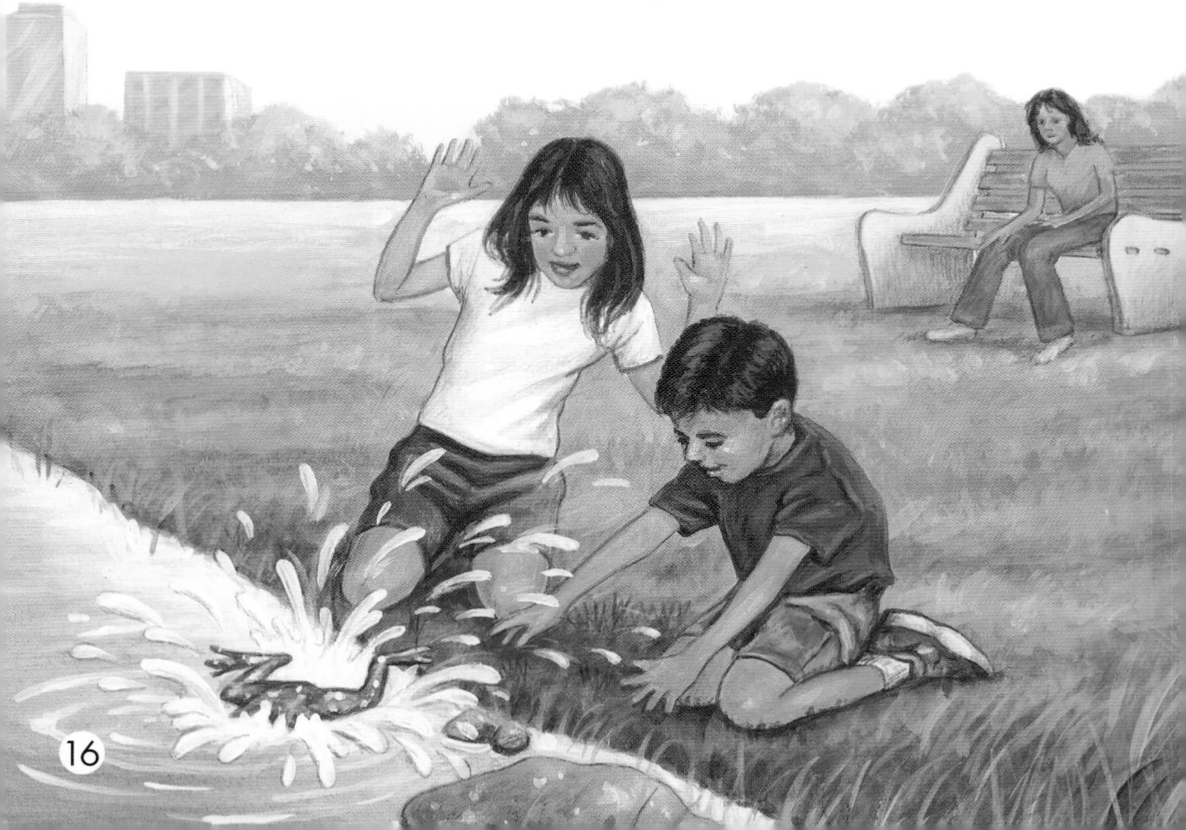